DECORATIVE
FUSION
KNOTS

A Step-by-Step Illustrated Guide to New and Unusual Ornamental Knots

DECORATIVE FUSION KNOTS

A Step-by-Step Illustrated Guide to New and Unusual Ornamental Knots

Written and Photographed by
JD of *Tying It All Together*

Green Candy Press

Fusion Knots — Innovative knots created through the merging of different knot elements or knotting techniques.

Decorative Fusion Knots
by J.D. Lenzen
ISBN 978-1-931160-78-0

Published by Green Candy Press
www.greencandypress.com

Design: Ian Phillips

Printed in Canada by Transcontinental Printing Inc.
Massively distributed by P.G.W.

Contents

Foreword

JD first came to my attention when he started to post on the web forum of the International Guild of Knot Tyers (IGKT), giving links to his videos on YouTube. These videos are impressive demonstrations of his knotting ability and provide astonishingly clear instructions on how to tie a variety of knots. But when it comes to knot books, there are many. And the vast majority of them show the same knots, albeit with different pictures and variations on how they can be tied.

So why choose this book?

First, it relies on step-by-step, clear, and easy to follow photographs rather than illustrated diagrams. Second, most of these knots have never appeared in books before. And further, this book not only teaches, it inspires!

Fusion knots show what can be achieved with a little patience and imagination, and provide endless opportunities for decorative knotting enjoyment. This is especially exciting for those who may have thought knots were something only used by specialists, such as sailors or climbers; or taught to Scouts and Guides, but then forgotten in the modern world of snaps and fasteners.

So while away a few minutes (and don't be surprised when hours have passed!). Tie some or all of these creations. All you need is a piece of cord, a little time, and a mind set to wonder.

Barry Mault
Honorary Secretary
International Guild of Knot Tyers
www.igkt.net

Acknowledgments

For their support and/or inspiration in the production of this book, I would like to thank Andrew McBeth, Cleo Dubois, Clifford W. Ashley, Bright Winn, Eve Minax, Sylvain Niles, my parents (Jim and Barbara) and all those who subscribe to my Tying It All Together YouTube channel. Without you, especially those who continue to support my online videos, this book would not have come to be.

And…a very special thanks to my wife and my muse, Kristen Kakos. Your presence in my life brings me joy, comfort, and the freedom to create. For these gifts I am forever grateful.

Introduction

For tens of thousands of years, knots played a critical role in human society. They have helped us catch food, sail the seas, build empires, worship, remember and heal. Quietly supporting us through all our historic conquests and adventures, knots helped our ancestors tie their world together.

The Incas of South America, for instance, may have used knots tied along strings as an early form of writing— communicating narratives of the Incan Empire through knots rather than ink and paper. They also used knots as accounting tools, generating and keeping records similar to those kept by modern day bookkeepers and census takers.

More popularly, the Celts used stylized representations of knots to express a variety of natural and spiritual concepts. Seen on ancient structures and in modern motifs, these decorative knots conveyed the relationships between man and woman, hunter and prey, earth, spirit and the universe. Still other Celtic knots are believed to have represented protection from evil spirits, and were placed on battle shields or near people who were sick.

Asian cultures, primarily Chinese, produced decorative knots that took on the esthetic qualities of religious symbols, nature and money. The Double Coin Knot, for instance, is so named because it looks like two Chinese coins overlapping. The majority of these decorative knots were meant to represent good luck, virtue, or prosperity. But others were created for more utilitarian purposes such as buttons for jackets and shirts.

Much like the development of any art form, time and practice are the keys to new ideas and innovative developments. Mariners throughout history, with lots of time of their hands, began coxcombing, covering rails and wheels with decorative wraps and ties. These wraps and ties served the dual purpose of improving the grip on an otherwise slippery object, while at the same time increasing the beauty of the ship.

As still more time passed, knots grew to become a semi-finite field of study. Knot books started presenting what had come before; with the most attention being paid to practical knots. Then, in 1944, Clifford W. Ashley published *The Ashley Book of Knots (ABOK)*, an encyclopedic reference manual describing how to tie thousands of decorative and functional knots from all around the world. To this day, Ashley's tome remains the quintessential book of knots.

Members of the International Guild of Knot Tyers (IGKT; officially founded in 1982) updated *ABOK* in 1979, adding what was then believed to be a new knot called the Hunter's Bend. Many of the guild members have gone on to write multiple books on the subject of knots. Most of these books, with the exception of a select few, focus on what has come before as opposed to new or recently created knots. When it comes to decorative knots, this last statement is especially true.

Introduction

So where do we go from here?

What does the future hold for knots?

The answer to both these questions, I believe, is fusion knots: innovative knots created through the merging of different knot elements or knotting techniques.

Like origami figurines created through the folding of paper, rope in the hands of a fusion knot tyer becomes a vehicle for exploring ever more complex and imaginative knot designs. Fusion knot tyers gather inspiration from history, nature, mythology, or any other source that moves them to tie. They see knots as assemblages of discrete parts, rather than indivisible units of information.

For instance, the Celtic Tree of Life Knot (a fusion knot) is the result of combining three different knot elements—one derived from the Trinity Knot, one from the Ring of Coins, and one from the Handbasket Knot. Together, these three elements commingle to create something different, something more elaborate and impactful.

This book is an introduction to the world of decorative fusion knots, but more so it is a bridge between what is and what can be. In turn, alongside fusion knots, I present instructions for historical knots, knots that were discovered or created before 1979 (the year the IGKT updated *ABOK*). Historical knots are the foundations for and elements of fusion knots, so knowing how to tie them is important.

In a few cases the historical knot instructions shown will not be presented as elements to subsequent fusion knots. The purpose for this is twofold:

A) I want to provide instructions for an unusual or rarely described historical knot, and

B) I want to provide techniques you can use to create fusion knots of your own.

The chapters of this book are organized according to the primary knot element or knotting technique utilized in the knot's construction. For example, if a knot starts off as a Double Coin Knot, but finishes with a technique associated with the Trinity Knot (as seen in the Djinn Bottle Knot), that knot will be placed in the Double Coin Knot chapter.

All this said, please remember, fusion knotting is a creative endeavor. Although the pages before you show a multitude of step-by-step instructions on how to tie knots, you do not have to be a passive consumer of this information. Modify what is shown, play with the techniques, integrate different knot elements, and create something new. Put another way…

Explore, Discover, Innovate!

Doing so will not only improve your understanding of fusion knots; it will improve your understanding of all knots and pave the way to ever more elaborate and creative knots tomorrow.

Thank you and keep tying.

— JD of Tying It All Together

Rope Orientation

The following definitions and visual clarifications are meant to provide an understanding of the terms and knotting procedures associated with this book.

Note: All the knots in this book were tied with a six foot length of ¼ inch solid braid nylon or equivalent lengths of paracord.

Definitions

Ascending End: The end of a line (usually the running end) going up.

Bight: A line doubled over into a **U**-shape.

Circle: A line making one complete revolution around another line.

Clockwise Loop: A loop that has a running end (or line on top) that rotates clockwise.

Counterclockwise Loop: A loop that has a running end (or line on top) that rotates counterclockwise.

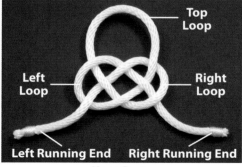

Rope Parts

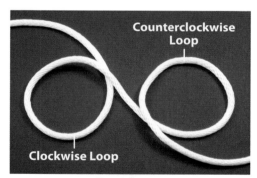

Rope Loops

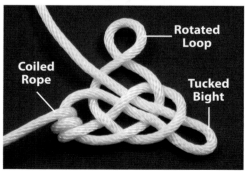

Knot Movements

Knot Parts

Rope Orientation

Coil: A line that makes several (more than one) revolutions around another line.

Crook: The curved part of a bight, circle or loop.

Flip: Turning a knot or semi-completed knot upside down.

Firm: The point at which the adjusting of a knot results in a satisfactory appearance.

Fusion Knot: An innovative knot created through the merging of different knot elements or knotting techniques.

Historical Knot: Knots that were discovered or created before 1979 (the year the IGKT updated *ABOK*).

Hook: A line that makes a sharp curve or a shape resembling a hook.

Knot Component: A knot element or knotting technique used to make a fusion knot.

Line: The material used to tie a knot (e.g., rope, paracord, wire, etc.)

Loop: A circle of line that crosses itself.

P: A line that is looped to look like the letter **P** or the mirror image of the letter **P**.

Pentaradial: Lines or knots splayed out in a configuration characteristic of echinoderms (i.e., sea stars, sea urchins and sea cucumbers). Similar in appearance to a pentagon.

Rotate: To turn a loop 180 degrees around an axis.

Running End: The end of a line that's being used to make the knot.

Singe: Scorching the end of a cut line to hold it in place and keep it from fraying.

Standing End: The end of a line that is not involved in making the knot.

Tuck: Inserting a line or bight through a loop or under another line.

Weave: Passing a line over and under another line.

Y-Configuration: An arrangement of bights and running ends in the shape of the letter **Y**.

Flipping the Double Coin

Double Coin Knot

A decorative variant of the Carrick Bend, the Double Coin Knot's structure and elegant simplicity make it the perfect base for multiple fusion knots. This was the knot that introduced me to the world of decorative knots.

Knot Components: Historical Knot

1. Make a clockwise **P** with the ascending rope on top the loop created.

2. Drop the right running end down over the loop of the **P**.

3. Bight the running end and weave it under the "leg" of the **P**, over…

4. …the rope above it, under the top of the **P**, and then over itself.

5. Tuck the bight under the bottom of the **P**.

6. Pull the running end out until the knot is firm.

Cloud Knot

The Cloud Knot branches off the Double Coin Knot in an innovative and seldom realized way. The knot is created via a weaving technique that can be applied to a variety of knots, making them appear more elaborate.

Knot Components: Double Coin Knot + Opposing Weaves

1. Begin by tying a Double Coin Knot.

2. Untuck the right running end of the knot.

3. Then, untuck the left running end of the knot.

4. Weave the left running end under, over, and under the right ropes.

5. Weave the right running end under, over, under, and over the left ropes.

6. Carefully adjust the knot until firm.

Djinn Bottle Knot

The Arabian Nights Entertainments tells of a djinn that is imprisoned in a bottle for 1,800 years. When the djinn is released, it grants wishes. The Djinn Bottle Knot calls to this story, representing the djinn's prison vessel in rope.

Knot Components: Double Coin Knot + Trinity Knot

1. Begin by tying a Double Coin Knot.

2. Stretch the knot's top loop out about 1½ inches.

3. Cross the right running end over the left and…

4. … tuck it under and out the left loop.

5. Tuck the other running end over and through the right loop.

6. Rotate the top loop (left rope over right).

7. Cross the right running end over the top loop.

8. Weave the left running end under the outer edge of the top loop,…

9. …and then over, and under the ropes above it at a diagonal.

10. Carefully adjust the knot until firm.

Prosperity Knot

Denoting abundance and long life, the Prosperity Knot is said to bring wealth, in all its manifestations, to those who tie or incorporate it into their attire. Be this fact or fiction, the knot's beauty is unquestionable.

Knot Components: Historical Knot

1. Begin by tying a Double Coin Knot.

2. Then stretch the left and right loops out about two inches.

3. Drop the loops so that they're below the left and right running ends.

4. Rotate both loops (left rope over right).

5. Tuck the loop on the left through the back of the loop on the right.

6. Drop the right running end down across the right loop.

7. Weave the left loop over the running end and under the right loop.

8. Weave the left running end under the outer edge of the left loop,…

9. …and then over, under, over, and…

10. …under the ropes below it at a diagonal. Adjust the knot until firm.

Wide Lanyard Knot

The Wide Lanyard Knot looks like a Prosperity Knot turned on its side. A historical knot that has been around since at least the 19th century, it is also the fusion of the Double Coin Knot and Panel Knot.

Knot Components: Historical Knot

1. Begin by tying a Double Coin Knot.

2. Then bight the right running end back and beside itself.

3. Bight the left running end back and beside itself as well.

4. Pull out and split the running ends apart from one another.

5. Hook the left running end down, diagonally across the knot.

6. Drop the right running end down, over the left.

7. Continue forward, weaving the running end under,…

8. …over, under, and over the ropes below it at a diagonal.

9. Weave the other running end over, under, over, and…

10. …under the rope below it at a diagonal. Adjust the knot until firm.

Mayan Temple Knot

Archaeological evidence suggests the ancient Mayans first began building their stepped temples about 3,000 years ago. The Mayan Temple Knot, on the other hand, is new to the world; still I hope it lasts just as long.

Knot Components: Wide Lanyard Knot + Keyhole Weave

1. Begin by tying a Double Coin Knot.

2. Then bight the right running end back and beside itself.

3. Bight the left running end back and beside itself as well.

4. Circle the right running end forward around the top loop.

5. Circle the left running end back around the top loop.

6. Continue weaving the left running end over and under the ropes…

7. …below it. Then over, under, and over the ropes at a diagonal.

8. Weave the right running end under and over the ropes below it.

9. Then under, over, and…

10. …under the ropes below it at a diagonal. Adjust the knot until firm.

River Knot

The River Knot is an expansion of the Double Coin Knot that results in the appearance of the sun rising over a rippling river. Valued for its riparian beauty and graceful weaves, this knot is one of my personal favorites.

Knot Components: Historical Knot

1. Begin by tying a Double Coin Knot.

2. Make a counterclockwise **P** with the right running end.

3. Tuck the right running end through the right Double Coin Knot loop.

4. Make a clockwise **P** with the left running end.

5. Tuck the left running end through the left Double Coin Knot loop.

6. Weave the left running end under, over, and…

7. …under the ropes above it.

8. Hook the running end to the right and continue under, over, and under.

9. Now weave the right running end under the rope to its left,…

10. …then over, under, and over the ropes above it.

11. Hook the running end to the left and continue over, under, and over.

12. Adjust the knot until it takes on its distinctive appearance.

Ring of Coins

The Ring of Coins is a compound knot, a string of knots tied together in series or a cluster. Knots brought together in such a way create complex configurations that have been treasured and admired for centuries.

Knot Components: Historical Knot

1. Begin by tying a Double Coin Knot.

2. Untuck the right running end.

3. Weave the running end through the back of the right loop,…

4. …then over and under the ropes to the right. Leave a three inch loop.

5. Make a clockwise loop over the right edge of the three inch loop.

6. Insert the right running end through the front of the small loop…

7. …then weave it under, over, and under the ropes below it.

8. Now, untuck the left running end.

9. Weave the running end through the front of the left loop,…

10. …then under and over the ropes to the left. Leave a three inch loop.

11. Make a clockwise loop under the left edge of the three inch loop.

12. Insert the left running through the back of the small loop,…

13. …then weave it over, under, and over the ropes below it.

14. Untuck the right running end.

15. Untuck the left running end.

16. Cross the right running end over the left.

17. Insert the left running end through the back of the lower right loop.

18. Hook the running end up, weaving it over and under the ropes to the left.

19. Insert the right running end through the front of the lower left loop.

20. Hook the running end up, weaving it under and over the ropes to the right.

21. Cross the right running end over the left.

22. Then weave it under and over the ropes below it at a diagonal.

23. Weave the other running end over and under the ropes below it at a diagonal.

24. Carefully adjust the knot until firm.

Section 2

Opening
the Box

Box Knot

The Box Knot is arguably the simplest way to create a square or "box" formation with rope. The base for multiple other knots, it is also attractive on its own—its simplicity stealing nothing of its beauty.

Knot Components: Historical Knot

1. Make a counterclockwise loop (right rope over left).

2. Tuck the rope on the right up behind the loop at a diagonal.

3. Hook the rope on the lower left up, over, under, and over the ropes above it.

4. Then drop it down through the back of the right loop.

5. Drop the rope on the left down through the front of the left loop.

6. Carefully adjust the knot until firm.

Jolly Roger Knot

Jolly Roger pirate flags were most commonly skull and crossbones, but in truth there were several different pirate flags. The Jolly Roger Knot emulates one that displayed a skull wearing a tri-cornered hat.

Knot Components: Box Knot + Double Coin Knot + Rotated Loops

1. Begin by tying a Box Knot.

2. Then stretch the left and right loops out about one inch.

3. Below the Box Knot tie a Double Coin Knot in reverse. Using…

4. …a counterclockwise **P** and dropping the running end behind it.

5. Flip the piece upside down.

6. Rotate the left loop, top over bottom.

7. Insert the left running end through the back of the left loop.

8. Rotate the right loop, bottom over top.

9. Insert the right running end through the front of the right loop.

10. Carefully adjust the knot until firm.

Olias Knot

The Olias Knot was inspired by the symbol shown on the cover art of Jon Anderson's progressive rock concept album, *Olias of Sunhillow*. The symbol and the knot represent the unity between the earthly and the divine.

Knot Components: Box Knot + Opposing Weaves

1. Begin with Step 3 of the Box Knot.

2. Drop the left and right running ends over and behind the loops.

3. Weave the left running end over, under, and over the right ropes.

4. Then weave the right running end over,…

5. …under, over, and…

6. …under the left ropes. Carefully adjust the knot until firm.

Harbin Knot

Harbin Hot Springs is the place I go to when seeking rest and peace of mind. During one of my visits I was fiddling with rope and came up with the following knot. The knot's name is an homage to the place of its creation.

Knot Components: Box Knot + Ring of Coins + Rotated Loops

1. Begin with Step 3 of the Box Knot.

2. Then stretch the left and right loops out about one inch.

3. Drop the left and right running ends down over and behind the loops.

4. Cross the left running end over the right.

5. Rotate the right loop, top over bottom.

6. Now insert the running end on the right over the right loop's crook.

7. Weave it forward under and over the ropes above it at a diagonal,…

8. …then pinch it back to the right. Rotate the left loop, bottom over top.

9. Insert the running end on the left up and over the left loop's crook.

10. Weave it forward over and under the ropes above it at a diagonal.

11. Cross the right running end over all the ropes below it at a diagonal.

12. Tuck it down above the crook of the lowest left loop.

13. Cross the left running end over,…

14. …under, and…

15. …over the ropes below it at a diagonal.

16. Carefully adjust the knot until firm.

Snake Weave

As the name implies, the Snake Weave is evocative of two snakes slithering back and forth across one another. This action creates a decorative strap that can be as long, or as short, as you wish.

Knot Components: Historical Knot

1. Begin with Step 3 of the Box Knot. Then turn it upside down.

2. Stretch the bottom loop to the length you want the Snake Weave to be.

3. Rotate the bottom loop (left rope over right).

4. Then drop the rope on the right down across the bottom loop.

5. Weave the rope on the left under, over, and under the ropes.

6. Repeat Steps 3 through 5 until you can no longer rotate loops.

Dagger Knot

Daggers are weapons used for thrusting and cutting. The Dagger Knot, however, is useless at both. A Snake Weave with a twist, the knot is purely decorative. But don't let this fact keep you from taking a stab at it.

Knot Components: Snake Weave + Circled Opposing Loops

1. Begin with a Snake Weave about two inches long.

2. Stretch the bottom loop of the Snake Weave out about four inches.

3. Lift the rope on the right up and over the top of the loop.

4. Circle the rope around the loop and over itself.

5. Then tuck the rope on the left under the bottom of the loop.

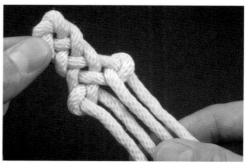

6. Circle the rope around the loop and under itself.

7. Cross the rope on the left over the right, exiting under the loop.

8. Lift the rope on the left up and over the top of the loop.

9. Rotate the bottom loop (left rope over right).

10. Begin "Snake Weaving" until…

11. …you can no longer rotate loops.

12. Adjust the knot until firm. Flip it around to see the dagger.

Celtic Bar

The Celtic Bar is a woven bight version of the Snake Weave, and makes a great wrist band, belt, luggage tag, or strap for a bag. Still, in all truth, your imagination is the only thing that limits its application.

Knot Components: Snake Weave + Woven Bights

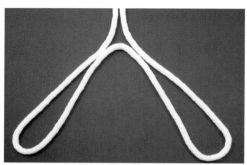

1. Create a **Y**-configuration of two bights branching off a doubled rope.

2. Cross the rope ends right over left.

3. Drop both rope ends, then cross the left rope over the right.

4. Drop both bights, thencross the left bight over the right.

5. Repeat Steps 3 and 4,…

6. …weaving back and forth…

7. …until you can no longer…

8. …cross the rope ends.

9. Insert the rope end on the right into the front of its adjacent bight.

10. Insert the rope end on the left into the back of its adjacent bight.

11. Turn the bar onto its side.

12. Now insert the left rope into the front…

13. …of its opposing bight.

14. Then insert the right rope into the front…

15. …of its opposing bight.

16. Carefully adjust the knot until firm.

Section 3

Weaving and Tucking Bights

Half Good Luck Knot

A good friend of mine is fond of saying, "It's called the Half Good Luck Knot because people need good luck to tie it." With all due respect, this couldn't be further from the truth. Elegantly designed, the knot slides together easily.

Knot Components: Historical Knot

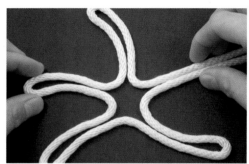

1. Make a pentaradial formation of four bights off two running ends.

2. Cross the running ends over the first bight.

3. Cross the first bight over the running ends and the second bight.

4. Cross the second bight over the first and the third bight.

5. Cross the third bight over the second and the fourth bight.

6. Cross the fourth bight over the third bight and into the crook above it.

Spiral Knot

The Spiral Knot is essentially a Good Luck Knot with a twist! Utilizing three "arms" instead of five, the knot adds hooked turns and extra weaves to create its triple spiral configuration.

Knot Components: Good Luck Knot + Hooked Turns + Extra Weaves

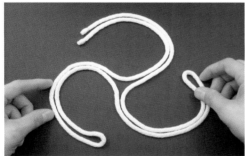

1. Create a **Y**-configuration of two bights swirling off a doubled rope.

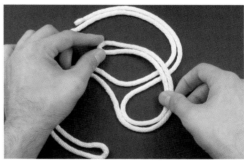

2. Hook the lower bight counterclockwise and over the running ends.

3. Hook the running ends counterclockwise and over the upper bight.

4. Hook the upper bight counterclockwise, over the running ends, and…

5. …into the crook of the lower bight.

6. Now tighten the bights and rope ends loosely.

7. Weave the lower bight counterclockwise, under, and…

8. …through the crook of the swirl above it.

9. Repeat Steps 7 and 8 for the upper bight, but use the swirl below it.

10. Finally, weave the running ends counterclockwise, under, and…

11. …through the crook of the swirl to its right.

12. Carefully adjust the knot until firm.

Triskelion Knot

A triskelion is a symbol consisting of three interlocking spirals or any similar symbol with three protrusions and a threefold rotational symmetry. The Triskelion Knot mimics this historic configuration.

Knot Components: Good Luck Knot + Looped Ends

1. Create a **Y**-configuration of two bights swirling off a doubled rope.

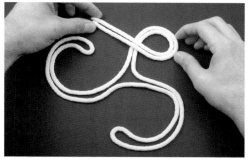

2. Loop the running ends clockwise over themselves.

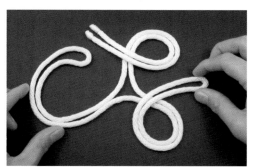

3. Loop the right bight clockwise over it self.

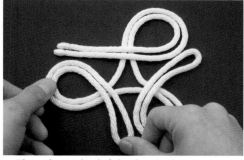

4. Then, loop the left bight clockwise over itself.

5. Insert the tip of the right bight through the upper loop.

6. Insert the tip of the left bight through the right loop.

7. Insert the running ends through the left loop.

8. Carefully adjust the knot until…

9. …its running ends and bights sprout firmly from a threefold center.

10. Flip the knot over to see the triskelion.

Tea Cup Knot

The Tea Cup Knot is a product of my explorations into three dimensional knots. Starting off as a variant of the Good Luck Knot, the knot's finishing technique makes it so much more!

Knot Components: Good Luck Knot + Hooked Turns + Extra Weaves + Shaping

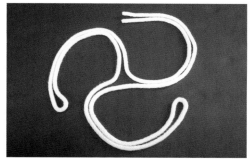

1. Create a **Y**-configuration of two bights swirling off a doubled rope.

2. Hook the running ends counterclockwise over the upper bight's crook.

3. Hook the upper bight counterclockwise over the lower bight's crook.

4. Hook the lower bight counterclockwise over the running end's crook.

5. Tuck the bight on the top under and through the crook to the left,…

6. …then over and under the doubled ropes below it.

7. Repeat Steps 5 and 6 for the running ends…

8. …to the left.

9. Then repeat Steps 5 and 6 again, for the bight…

10. …on the bottom.

11. Flip the knot over. Then firm it up by pulling on the loose ends.

12. Fold the running ends over in front of the upper bight.

13. Fold the upper bight over in front of the lower bight.

14. Insert the lower bight through the crook of the running ends.

15. Pull on the loose ends until firm, and then cut them off at their bases.

16. While bracing the knot, push your thumbs into its center,…

17. …pulling up the knot's sides as you do.

18. Carefully adjust the knot until firm.

Panel Knot

The Panel Knot is a lovely knot on its own. This said, it is also a tying technique that can be incorporated into a variety of other knots, creating larger more elaborate configurations.

Knot Components: Historical Knot

1. Drop a counterclockwise loop about three inches long.

2. Tuck the right running end down to create a bight.

3. Weave the running end up under, over, and under the ropes above.

4. Weave the running end down alongside itself.

5. Weave the running end up under, over, under,…

6. …over, and under the ropes above.

7. Repeat Step 4.

8. Then weave the running end up under, over, under,…

9. …over, under, over, and under the ropes above.

10. Carefully adjust the knot until firm.

Longhorn Knot

Evocative of the head and horns of Texas cattle, the Longhorn Knot is a strikingly attractive tie. Beautiful on its own or as an element in a larger piece, its graceful shape makes it a great base for a collar or necklace.

Knot Components: Panel Knot + Rotated Bights

1. Make an Overhand Knot, the right running end weaving over the left.

2. Tuck the left running end down to create a bight.

3. Tuck the right running end down to create a second bight.

4. Bight the left running end up, weaving it under, over, and under.

5. Hook the right running end over and through the lower left bight.

6. Now weave the right running end over, under, and over.

7. Adjust the knot until the upper left and right bights stick out.

8. Rotate the right bight, top over bottom, to create a loop.

9. Insert the right running end through the back of the loop created.

10. Rotate the left bight, bottom over top, to create a second loop.

11. Insert the left running end through the front of the second loop created.

12. Adjust the knot until it takes on its distinctive appearance.

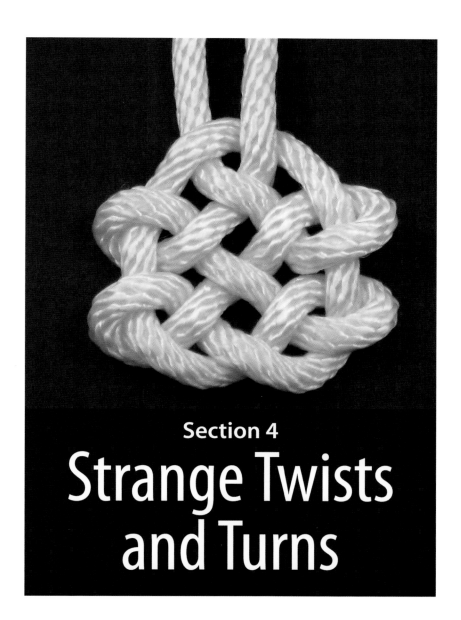

Strange Twists and Turns

Pendant Knot

Born of the desire to create a simple yet elegant accessory to a necklace, the Pendant Knot has more than proven its worth. Several knots, in fact, owe at least part of their beauty to this tying technique.

Knot Components: Circled Opposing Loops

1. Make a clockwise loop (bottom rope over top).

2. Hook the ascending running end left, creating a "pretzel."

3. Then circle it around the back of the loop and behind itself, exiting in front.

4. Circle the other end around the front of the loop and over itself, exiting in back.

5. Cross the left running end over the right.

6. Repeat Step 3.

7. Repeat Step 4.

8. Repeat Step 5.

9. Finish the piece by tucking the left running end under the loop.

10. Adjust the knot until firm. Flip it over to see the pendant.

Challenge Knot

The Challenge Knot's name is derived from the focus that must be undertaken during its creation. More to the point, tying the knot will test both patience and ability. Still, its beauty makes the challenge of its formation well worth it.

Knot Components: Historical Knot

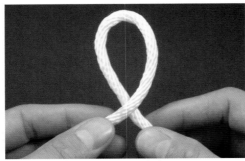

1. Make a clockwise loop (left rope over right).

2. Flip the crossed running ends up and over the top of the loop.

3. Cross the left running end over the right, and…

4. …tuck it under the loop. This will create a left and right loop.

5. Slide the left loop over the right loop.

6. Distend the left and right loops, creating a figure eight between them.

7. Rotate the left loop clockwise (bottom rope over top).

8. Rotate the right loop clockwise (top rope over bottom).

9. Now weave the left running end under...

10. ...over, under and over the ropes below it at a diagonal.

11. Weave the right running end over, under, over, and...

12. ...under the ropes below it at a diagonal. Adjust the knot until firm.

Basket Weave Knot

The Basket Weave Knot is deceivingly similar in appearance to the Prosperity Knot, with two major exceptions, it's easier to tie and adjust. My hope is that you'll find the knot an elegant addition to your growing knowledge of rectangular flat knots.

Knot Components: Historical Knot

1. Make a clockwise loop (left rope over right).

2. Create an Overhand Knot and drop it down about three inches.

3. Lift the running ends and pull the loops created apart.

4. Rotate both loops (left rope over right).

5. Tuck the left loop under the right.

6. Weave the right running end over…

7. …under-under, and over the ropes below it at a diagonal.

8. Then weave the left running end under, over, under,…

9. …over, and under the ropes below it at a diagonal.

10. Carefully adjust the knot until firm.

Brigid's Knot

Christians believe Brigid of Kildare a saint. Pagans believe her a goddess. Both exalt her beauty and immeasurable kindness. Brigid's Knot represents this legendary woman by intertwining her symbol (a woven cross) with an open heart.

Knot Components: Basket Weave Knot + Circled Opposing Loops + Keyhole Weave

1. Drop a two inch counterclockwise loop (left rope over right).

2. Circle the running end around the rope, and through the loop.

3. One inch from the first loop, drop a second equal sized clockwise loop.

4. Circle the running end around the rope, and through the loop.

5. Cross the right running end over the left.

6. Weave the other running end over and through the loop on the right.

7. Weave the rope on the left under and through the loop on the left.

8. Cross the right loop over the left.

9. Weave the left running end over, under, and over the ropes below it.

10. Weave the right running end under, over, and…

11. …under the ropes below it.

12. Adjust the knot until firm. Flip it around to see the cross and heart.

Handbasket Knot

Possessing the same silhouette as the Cloud Knot, the Handbasket Knot nevertheless stands alone. Based upon a Celtic design I saw drawn on a historic motif, the knot has since been incorporated into multiple fusion knots.

Knot Components: Historical Knot

1. Make a counterclockwise loop (right rope over left).

2. Rotate the loop counterclockwise, creating a twist.

3. Rotate the twist up into the center of the loop above.

4. Tuck the left running end underneath the left edge of the loop.

5. Hook the right running end down, over the right edge of the loop…

6. …under-under, and over the left edge of the loop.

7. Hook the left running end down over, under, over, under,…

8. …over, under, and over the ropes below it horizontally.

9. Carefully adjust the knot,…

10. …stretching the top loop to generate the look of a handbasket.

Deconstructing the Trinity

Trinity Knot

The Trinity Knot can be found on Celtic motifs throughout the British Isles. The design was also used by ancient Germans and Romans. Generally speaking, it's a symbol of things and persons that are threefold.

Knot Components: Historical Knot

1. Make three counterclockwise loops (right ropes over left).

2. Cross the left running end over the right.

3. Then insert it up through the back of the right loop…

4. ..and across the back of the middle loop.

5. Weave the other running end through the front of the left loop,…

6. …then over, under, and over the ropes above it, at a diagonal.

Hammer Knot

During the era of the Vikings, miniature Thor's hammers were worn around the neck for good luck. The Hammer Knot resurrects this historic symbol, allowing the creation of a similarly shaped amulet made of rope.

Knot Components: Trinity Knot + Snake Weave + Circled Opposing Loops

1. Begin by tying a Trinity Knot.

2. Stretch the bottom loop of the Trinity Knot out about two inches.

3. Reverse the over under tuck of the left and right running ends.

4. Circle the right running end around the loop and over itself.

5. Take the left running end and…

6. …circle it around the loop, under itself, and…

7. …over the other running end.

8. Continue forward and tuck the running end under the loop.

9. Rotate the bottom loop (left rope over right).

10. Drop the rope on the right down across the bottom loop.

11. Weave the rope on the left under, over, and…

12. …under the ropes below it. Then carefully adjust the knot until firm.

Triple Goddess Knot

The triple goddess symbol of the waxing, full, and waning moon is believed to represent the characteristics of maiden, mother, and crone. The Triple Goddess Knot equally embodies these three stages of a woman's life.

Knot Components: Trinity Knot + Ring of Coins

1. Make a counterclockwise loop (right rope over left).

2. Then make a second counterclockwise loop to the right of the first.

3. Cross the right running end over the left.

4. Hook the rope on the right up through the back of the right loop.

5. Hook the rope on the left up through the front of the left loop.

6. Weave the rope on the left under, over, and…

7. …under the ropes below it, at a diagonal.

8. Weave the rope on the right under the top left rope, and over…

9. …under and over the ropes below it, at a diagonal.

10. Carefully adjust the knot until firm.

Cupcake Knot

I struggled for a long time over a name for this knot, finally settling on Cupcake Knot on account, well…it looks like a cupcake. So be it your birthday or simply time for a treat, this attractive morsel is yours for the tying.

Knot Components: Trinity Knot + Ring of Coins

1. Make a counterclockwise loop (right rope over left).

2. Then make a second counterclockwise loop to the right of the first.

3. Cross the left running end over the right.

4. Flip the piece upside down.

5. Drop the left and right running ends behind and over the loops.

6. Now cross the right running end over the left.

7. Hook and weave the rope on the right up and through…

8. …the loop on the right, then back over and under the ropes above it.

9. Now hook the other rope under the rope dangling in the back.

10. Then hook it right weaving it over, under, over,…

11. …under, over, and…

12. …under the ropes below it at a diagonal. Adjust the knot until firm.

Pentaradial Knot

The Pentaradial Knot was named on account of its similarity to the configuration of a bat star—a marine animal found along the Pacific coast of North America. Both the bat star and the knot are arranged along five rays of symmetry.

Knot Components: Trinity Knot + Basket Weave Knot

1. Make a counterclockwise loop (right rope over left).

2. Then make a second counterclockwise loop to the right of the first.

3. Cross the left running end over the right and bight it through the…

4. …back of the right loop. Do the same in reverse with the other rope end.

5. Flip the piece upside down.

6. Insert the left bight through the back of the right bight.

7. Wrap the right running end over and through its adjacent loop.

8. Drop the running end behind the first bight and over the second.

9. Tuck the first bight down under the far right edge of the second.

10. Wrap the left running end over and through its adjacent loop.

11. Weave the running end over, under,…

12. …over, and under the ropes below it. Adjust the knot until firm.

Celtic Tree of Life Knot

The Celtic tree of life symbolizes strength, longevity, and wisdom. It marks the connection between earth, the spirit world, and the universe. Often portrayed in illustration, it's rarely if ever shown in rope…until now.

Knot Components: Trinity Knot + Ring of Coins + Handbasket Knot

1. Make a counterclockwise loop (right rope over left).

2. Then make a second counterclockwise loop to the right of the first.

3. Cross the left running end over the right.

4. Flip the piece upside down.

5. Drop the left and right running ends behind and over the loops.

6. Weave the right running end up under, over, and under the ropes above.

7. Hook the left running end over and through the lower right loop.

8. Weave the left running end up over, under, and over the ropes above.

9. Hook the right running end under, over-over, and under the ropes.

10. Hook the left running end behind, over, and under the ropes…

11. …below it at a diagonal. Then over, under…

12. …over, and under the ropes ahead. Adjust the knot until firm.

Pagoda Knot

A pagoda is a tiered tower with multiple eaves. Common throughout eastern Asia, most pagodas were built to serve a religious function. The Pagoda Knot was created in admiration of this sacred architecture.

Knot Components: Trinity Knot + Opposing Weaves

1. Make a counterclockwise loop (right rope over left).

2. Make a second counterclockwise loop above the first.

3. Then a third loop to the right…

4. …and a fourth below.

5. Cross the left running end over the right.

6. Hook the rope on the right up through the back of the right loop.

7. Hook the rope on the left up through the front of the left loop.

8. Flip the piece upside down.

9. Drop the right running end down over the lower right loop.

10. Hook the left running end under, over, and under the ropes of the right loop.

11. Weave the other running end up under, then over…

12. …under, and over the ropes to the left. Flip the knot to see the Pagoda.

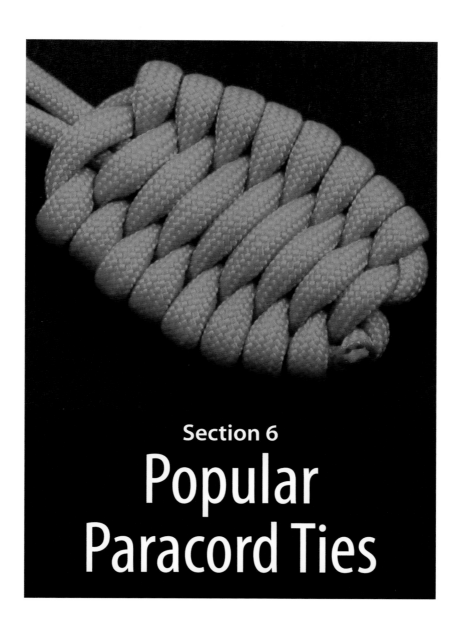

Section 6
Popular
Paracord Ties

Solomon Bar

Also called a Cobra Stitch and Portuguese Sinnet, the Solomon Bar is great way to bundle a lot of cord for later or emergency use. The firm strap created also makes it a popular tie for necklaces and bracelets.

Knot Components: Historical Knot

1. Begin by tying a Cow Hitch around a ring. Lower the ring to the…

2. …desired length of the bar. Insert the running ends into an upper ring.

3. Hook the right running end back, left, and over the left running end.

4. Hook the left running end right and through the right crook.

5. Hook the right running end left and under the left running end.

6. Hook the left running end back, right, and through the right crook.

7. Continue forward repeating Steps 3 and 4, and…

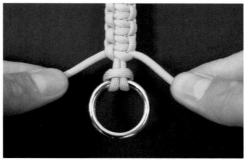

8. …Steps 5 and 6 until you reach the lower ring.

9. To finish the bar, carefully snip off the running ends…

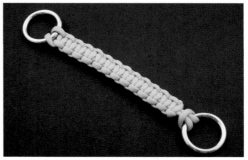

10. …and singe their ends to fix them in place.

Wide Solomon Bar

The Wide Solomon Bar is one of my favorite Paracord ties. Arguably the most durable and attractive looking strap a person can make; it is twice the width of a standard Solomon Bar. It also makes a great dog collar or stylish belt.

Knot Components: Solomon Bar + Crossed Cords

1. Begin by tying three Cow Hitches side-by-side around a ring.

2. Hook the right most rope left and under the third rope to the left.

3. Hook the third rope (to the left) back, right, and over the crook of the right most rope.

4. Hook the third rope right. Then hook the right most rope…

5. …under it, around the back, and over the crook of the third rope.

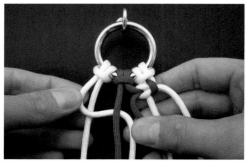

6. Hook the left most rope right and under the third rope to the right.

7. Hook the third rope (to the right) back, left, and over the crook of the left most rope.

8. Hook the third rope left. Then hook the left most rope…

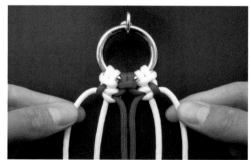

9. …under it, around the back, and over the crook of the third rope.

10. Cross the two parallel ropes in the middle, right over left.

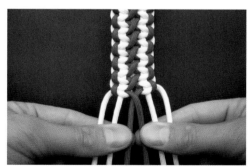

11. Repeat Steps 2 through 10 until the desired bar length is achieved.

12. To finish the bar carefully snip and singe the running ends.

Single Genoese Bar

The Single Genoese Bar is what happens when you tie alternating Half Hitches around a doubled rope. A simple design that forms a strong strap, it is sometimes confused with the Double Genoese Bar tied with alternating Clove Hitches.

Knot Components: Historical Knot

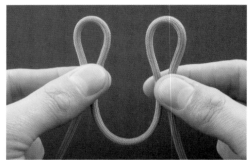

1. Branch a single strand of Paracord into two side-by-side bights.

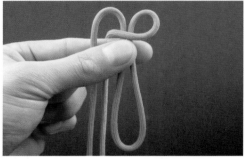

2. Hook the right running end left over the doubled rope…

3. …around the back and through the loop created. Tighten.

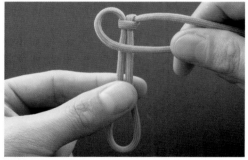

4. Hook the left running end right over the doubled rope,…

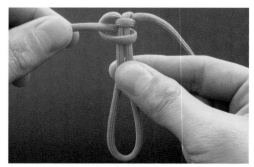

5. …around the back and through the loop created. Tighten.

6. Repeat Steps 2 and 3…

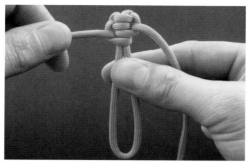

7. …and Steps 4 and 5…

8. …until you reach the desired length of your bar.

9. To finish the bar carefully snip and singe the running ends.

10. Cow Hitch the bar's loop to connect it to a bag or zipper.

Trilobite Knot

The Trilobite Knot is a tie most commonly used to create a key fob or a grip for a zipper. Tied in hand, the knot can be difficult to complete. But tying it off a hook, as shown below, makes it easier.

Knot Components: Historical Knot

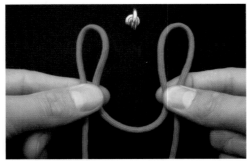

1. Create an **M**-shape with the rope, two bights with a trough between.

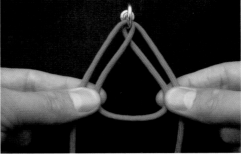

2. Loop the tops of the bights over a hook (left over right).

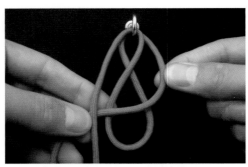

3. Hook the right running end left and under the left running end.

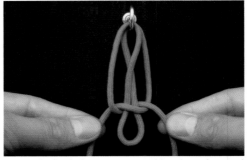

4. Hook the left running end back, right, and over the right crook.

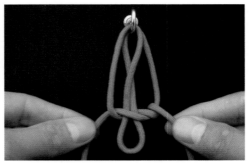

5. Circle one running end around the rope above it.

6. Circle the other running end around the rope above it.

7. Extend the left running end back, right, and over the right crook.

8. Extend the right running end left and under the left crook.

9. Repeat Step 5…

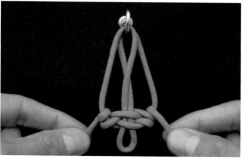

10. …and Step 6…

11. Continue forward repeating, Step 7…

12. …and Step 8, then Steps 5 and 6, back and forth until…

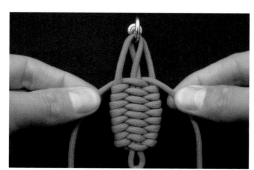

13. …you reach the desired length of your knot.

14. Then unhook the knot…

15. …and pull its bottom loop taut until firm.

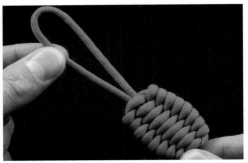

16. To finish the piece carefully snip and singe the running ends.

Petals of
the Flower

Flower Knot

The Flower Knot is sometimes called the Clover Leaf Knot. The technique used to create it can generate a variety of knots with loops or "petals" branching off a woven square center.

Knot Components: Historical Knot

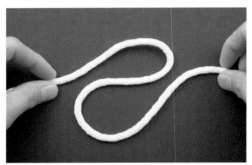

1. Make a **Z**-configuration of two opposing bights along the rope.

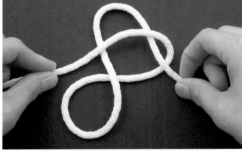

2. Bight the lower running end over and through the bight above.

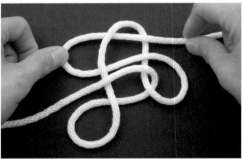

3. Now bight the running end over and through the bight created.

4. Hook the running end over and through the last bight created,…

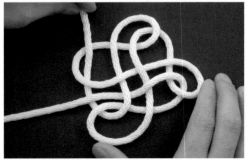

5. …through the bottom loop, and through the last bight created again.

6. Carefully adjust the knot until firm.

Double Looped Knot

The Double Looped Knot points out an important fact regarding the "petals" of the Flower Knot: you can make as many or as few as you'd like. So although the following shows how to size the knot down, you can just as easily size it up.

Knot Components: Historical Knot

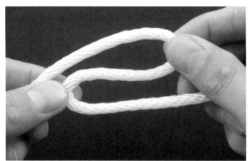

1. Make a **Z**-configuration of two opposing bights along the rope.

2. Bight the lower running end over and through the bight above.

3. Hook the running end over and through the last bight created…

4. …through the bottom loop, and through the last bight created again.

5. Carefully adjust the petals…

6. …until the knot is firm.

Cross Knot

The Cross Knot is essentially a Flower Knot with its petals pulled off. It can be used to fix the orientation of a whistle or pendant with an attractive cross or woven square, depending on which side of the knot is shown.

Knot Components: Historical Knot

1. Hook a bight around the rope beside it.

2. Circle the dangling rope up, over and around the bight.

3. Wrap the running end of the bight…

4. …around the dangling running end and through its crook.

5. Carefully adjust the knot until firm.

6. Flip the knot over to see the woven square.

Winged Cross Knot

Branching off a single length of rope rather than two ropes in parallel, the Winged Cross Knot adds flare to an otherwise simple Cross Knot. Only one word of caution, apply "wing" tension equally, or the knot will collapse.

Knot Components: Historical Knot

1. Hook the running end up and over a bight.

2. Insert the running end into the crook of the bight.

3. Hook the running end down through the back of the lower right bight.

4. Then hook it through the lower left loop and back through the bight.

5. Carefully adjust the knot until firm.

6. Flip the knot over to see the woven square.

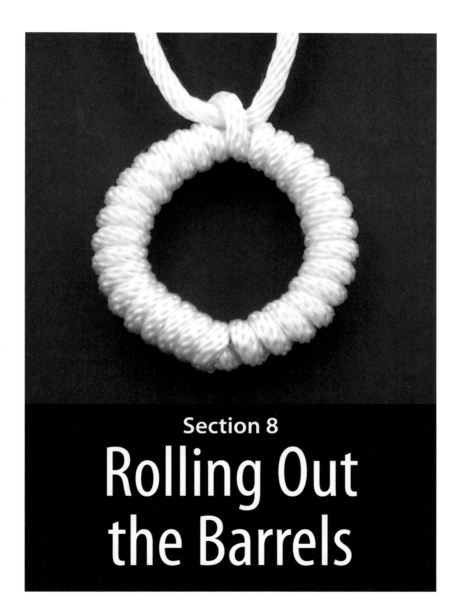

Section 8
Rolling Out the Barrels

Barrel Knot

The Barrel Knot is also called the Blood Knot because it was historically tied into the ends of cat-o'-nine-tails floggers. In contrast to its gruesome past, the knot also makes a clean, tight bead for decorating a necklace cord.

Knot Components: Historical Knot

1. Coil the rope three to four times around your index and middle finger.

2. Slide the coils off your fingers, while holding them in place.

3. Insert the right running end through the middle of the coils.

4. Insert the left running end through the middle of the coils.

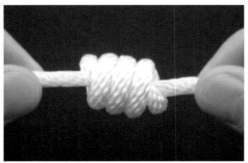

5. Gently pull the running ends in opposite directions until…

6. …a tightly wrapped bead of rope forms.

Bloody Knuckle Knot

The Bloody Knuckle Knot is what happens when you fuse a row of half hitches with the Blood Knot. The hitches make knuckles and the Blood Knot (or Barrel Knot) pulls the tie together, resulting in an unusual but attractive design.

Knot Components: Barrel Knot + Half Hitches

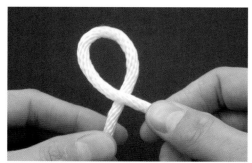

1. Make a counterclockwise loop (right rope over left).

2. Then make a second counterclockwise loop to the right of the first.

3. Place the second loop behind the first.

4. Repeat Steps 2 and 3…

5. …over and over again…

6. …until you have five loops lined up in front of one another.

7. Insert the right running end through the middle of the loops.

8. Insert the left running end through the middle of the loops.

9. Gently pull the running ends in opposite directions, and…

10. …carefully adjust the knot until firm.

O-Ring

The O-Ring is a quick way to make a sturdy decorative loop. Its convenient shape also makes it an ideal handle for a drawer, box lid, or tether.

Knot Components: Overhand Knot + Opposing Coils

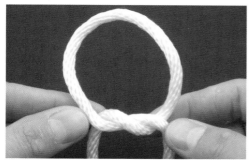

1. Make an Overhand Knot, the right running end weaving over the left.

2. Tightly coil the left running end around the loop, stopping at the top.

3. Repeat Step 2 for the right running end.

4. Pull the left and right running ends until all the coils of rope are tight.

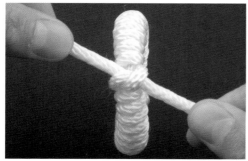

5. Tie an Overhand Knot to lock the piece in place.

6. Carefully adjust the ring until firm.

Door Knocker Knot

An actual door knocker helps people outside a house alert those inside of their presence. Despite its name, the Door Knocker Knot will only let others know of your knot tying prowess.

Knot Components: Historical Knot

1. Make an Overhand Knot, the right running end weaving over the left.

2. Rotate the loop of the Overhand Knot right over left.

3. Drop the right running end down behind the upper and bottom loop.

4. Circle the right running end through the bottom loop,…

5. … and up through the top right loop.

6. Then, circle the running end through the bottom and top loop again.

7. Repeat Steps 3 through 6 in reverse…

8. …until the left running end…

9. …circles through the top left and bottom loop twice.

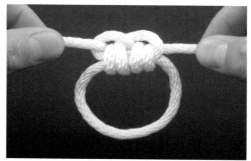

10. Carefully adjust the knot until firm.

Padlock Knot

The Padlock Knot is a clever way to achieve the look and function of a padlock. Still it should be noted, the knot is useless for protecting valuables. But then again, since the advent of bolt cutters, so are most padlocks.

*Knot Components: Opposing **P**s + Opposing Coils*

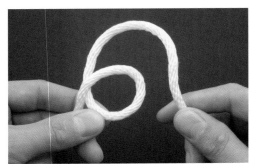

1. Make a counterclockwise **P** with the descending rope on top.

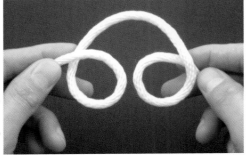

2. Make a second counterclockwise **P** facing the first.

3. Stack the first **P** on top of the second.

4. Circle the right running end around the ropes below it.

5. Circle the left running end around the ropes below it.

6. Repeat Step 4...

7. …and Step 5 until…

8. …both running ends coil around the ropes four to five times.

9. Hold the top loop and pull the running ends down to tighten.

10. To finish the knot carefully snip and singe the running ends.

Triple Barrel Knot

The Ashley Book of Knots describes the Triple Barrel Knot as merely one form of a variety of double looped knots. However, I feel the elegance of the knot's design deserves more specific attention, so I'm showing it here.

Knot Components: Historical Knot

1. Make a counterclockwise **P** about three inches down below the bight of the rope.

2. Then make a second counterclockwise **P** facing away from the first.

3. Cross the left running end over the right.

4. Insert the rope on the right through the front of the right loop.

5. Circle the rope around the right loop three times.

6. Insert the rope on the left through the back of the left loop.

7. Circle the rope around the left loop three times.

8. Make a counterclockwise loop with the top rope.

9. Then make a second counterclockwise loop on top of the first.

10. Insert the right running end through the back of the coils above.

11. Insert the left running end through the front of the coils above.

12. Flip the knot upside down and carefully adjust it until firm.

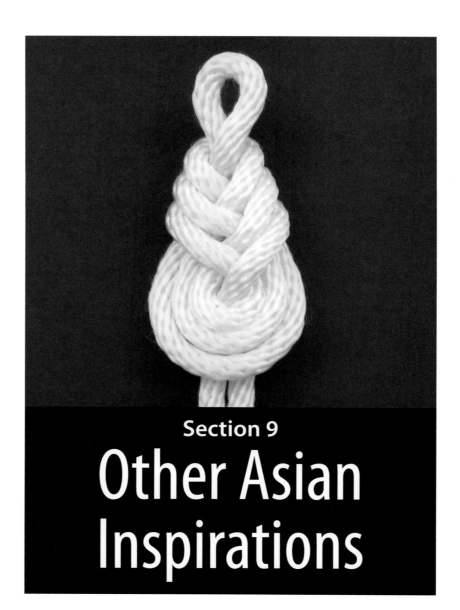

Section 9
Other Asian
Inspirations

Button Knot

The fundamental purpose of a Button Knot is its use as a button. However, this fact is occasionally sidestepped and its symbolic associations with good luck and the cyclical nature of all existence are emphasized.

Knot Components: Historical Knot

1. Make a clockwise **P**.

2. Drop the running end down behind the **P**, holding it in place.

3. Hook the other running end up, weaving it under, over,…

4. …under, and over the vertical ropes above it. Then hook it down,…

5. …weaving it over, under, over, and under the horizontal ropes above it.

6. Carefully adjust the knot until flat or a ball (flat configuration shown).

Maedate Knot

A maedate is a crest worn on the front of a samurai's helmet. Although most maedates were constructed of metal or horn, a handful of the earliest were constructed of rope. The Maedate Knot emulates their appearance.

Knot Components: Handcuff Knot + 180 Degree Rotation

1. Make a counterclockwise loop (right rope over left).

2. Then make a second counter-clockwise loop over the first.

3. Rotate the overlapping edges of the loops 180 degrees.

4. Pinch your thumbs and forefingers through the front and back loops.

5. Grip the rotated loops and pull them apart.

6. Carefully adjust the knot until firm.

Pipa Knot

The Pipa Knot's shape evokes the image of a Pipa—a stringed instrument dating back to ancient China. Greatly respected by Tang Dynasty poets, the Pipa was often praised in verse for its refined look and delicate tone.

Knot Components: Historical Knot

1. Make a clockwise loop (left rope over right).

2. Loop the rope on the left up around the back of the clockwise loop…

3. …and then back down across itself.

4. Repeat Steps 2 and 3, stacking each loop until…

5. …only a peephole remains in the center of the last loop created.

6. To firm up the knot, insert the running end into the peephole.

Plafond Knot

The Plafond Knot is named on account of its similarities to ceiling motifs in Chinese temples and palaces. A decorative way of holding two pieces of rope together, the knot also makes a striking rope medallion for a necklace.

Knot Components: Historical Knot

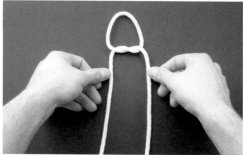

1. Make an Overhand Knot, the left running end weaving over the right.

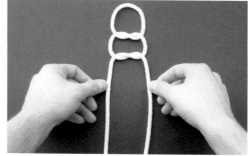

2. Repeat Step 1, one inch below the first knot.

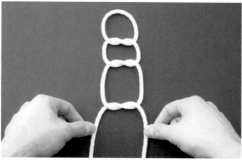

3. Repeat Step 1, two inches below the second knot.

4. Repeat Step 1 again, now one inch below the third knot.

5. Flip the forth Overhand Knot up over the third Overhand Knot.

6. Flip the top loop down, through the third and fourth knot centers.

7. Hook the left running end up, over the rope above it, and…

8. …through the second and first Overhand Knot centers.

9. Repeat Steps 7 and 8 for the right running end, but hook it up and under.

10. Carefully adjust the knot until firm.

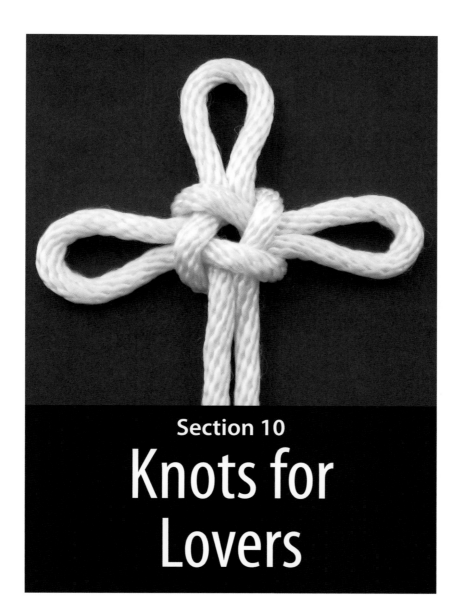

Knots for Lovers

True Lover's Knot

The True Lover's Knot has been a symbol of love, friendship, and affection since antiquity. Still, many distinct knots go by the same name, so it's not possible to say which one of them is, in fact, the truest of them all.

Knot Components: Historical Knot

1. Make a counterclockwise Overhand Knot, bottom over top.

2. Weave the opposing rope clockwise through the overhand loop,…

3. …around the back of, and then through itself.

4. Carefully split the left and right Overhand Knots. Then…

5. …pinch the intertwining center loops…

6. …and pull them apart until the knot is firm.

Kinky Lover's Knot

An alternative way of tying the True Lover's Knot, the Kinky Lover's Knot and its intertwining figure eights contribute to its unique appearance. Unexpectedly stunning when tied firmly, this is my kind of knot!

Knot Components: Historical Knot

1. Make a clockwise **P** with the ascending rope on top of the loop created.

2. Figure-eight the left running end through the back of the loop below.

3. Insert the right running through the back of the loop below.

4. Figure-eight the right running end through the upper left loop, around…

5. …the standing end and through the front of the lower right loop created.

6. Carefully adjust the knot until firm.

Clasped Hands Knot

Holding hands is one of the subtlest forms of physical contact two people can engage in. The Clasped Hands Knot replicates this elemental connection with coils circling the base of the Snake Knot.

Knot Components: Historical Knot

1. Make a clockwise **P**, hooking the running end to the right.

2. Insert the running end through the front of the **P**.

3. Hook the running end behind the leg of the **P** and through its front.

4. Carefully slide the ropes down to create the base for the Snake Knot.

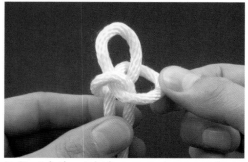

5. Stretch the right loop out about one inch.

6. Circle the right running end around the left, then through the right loop.

7. Repeat Step 6.

8. Turn the piece around 180 degrees so that the right side is on the left.

9. Repeat Step 6 two times, passing the right running end through…

10. …all the coils on the right. Carefully adjust the knot until firm.

Diamond Ring Knot

Now that you've completed nearly all the knots for lovers you're ready to tie the knot—the Diamond Ring Knot that is. A quick and clever combination of a triple Overhand Knot atop a dropped loop, the created ring "shines."

Knot Components: Overhand Knot + Circling

1. Make a counterclockwise **P**, hooking the running end to the right.

2. Insert the running end through the front of the **P**, creating an Overhand Knot.

3. Now circle it around and through the front of the Overhand Knot.

4. Allow a two inch loop to remain below.

5. Circle the running end around the top of the bottom loop,…

6. …over the top of the knot, and…

7. …through the double loops on the right.

8. Now circle it around and through the double loops, again.

9. Circle the other running end around and through the triple loops.

10. Then, carefully adjust the knot until firm.

Short and Long Sinnets

Eternity Knot

The Eternity Knot is an eye-catching way to decorate a rope or string. Suggestive of the Buddhist symbol for all-knowing wisdom, the knot can have spiritual significance as well.

Knot Components: Historical Knot

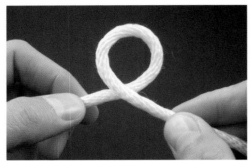

1. Make a counterclockwise loop (right rope over left).

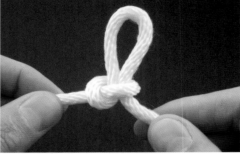

2. Bight the descending running end back through the loop and tighten.

3. Insert the running end into the bight created and tighten.

4. Now rotate the lower loop, top over bottom, to create a figure eight.

5. Insert the running end into the back of the lower figure eight loop.

6. Then carefully adjust the knot until firm.

Caterpillar Sinnet

Also called the Chain Sinnet, the Caterpillar Sinnet is an elegant rope chain tied with one leading end. The finished product can be used to make bracelets, necklaces or to store a long length of rope.

Knot Components: Historical Knot

1. Drop a clockwise loop (top rope over bottom).

2. Bight the running end, tuck it into the front of the loop and tighten.

3. Repeat Step 2…

4. …until you reach the desired length of your sinnet…

5. …or reach the end of your rope.

6. To finish the piece, insert the running end through the last loop and tighten.

Zipper Sinnet

I've been tying the Zipper Sinnet longer than any other knot in this book. First learned at camp when I was eight years old, the number of braclets I've made using this techniqe numbers into the hundreds.

Knot Components: Historical Knot

1. Make a counterclockwise loop (right rope over left).

2. Bight the right running end through the loop and tighten.

3. Bight the left running end through the first bight, and…

4. …tighten.

5. Repeat Step 2 and…

6. Steps 3 and 4, in series, again and again, until…

7. …your reach the desired length of your sinnet. To finish the piece…

8. …insert the running end into the last loop and…

9. …tighten.

10. Carefully adjust the sinnet until firm.

Spinal Sinnet

The Spinal Sinnet is fundamentally a chain of Eternity Knots. However, in contrast to its derivation, the sinnet takes on the look of a spinal column, with spinal cord and transverse processes represented.

Knot Components: Eternity Knot + Caterpillar Sinnet

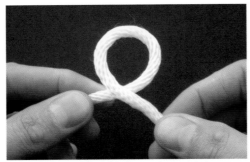

1. Make a counterclockwise loop (right rope over left).

2. Bight the descending running end through the loop and tighten.

3. Insert the running end into the bight created and tighten.

4. Rotate the lower loop, top over bottom, to create a figure eight.

5. Bight the running end into the back of the lower figure eight loop.

6. Repeat Step 3 through…

7. ...Step 5 until you reach the desired length of your sinnet.

8. To finish the piece, repeat Steps 3 and 4, then...

9. ...insert the running end through the back of the lower figure eight loop.

10. Flip the sinnet over to view its spine.

Bugle Cord

Bugle Cords are used as elaborate leashes on bugles and trumpets, and as ornamentation for band uniforms. Although relatively simple to make, there are a few subtle but important moves at the beginning of the tie, so take note.

Knot Components: Historical Knot

1. Fold the rope over on itself, drawing it down about twelve inches.

2. About three inches below the bight, circle the short end under…

3. …and around the long end, twice. The circles should move toward the bight.

4. Insert the short end back through the loops created.

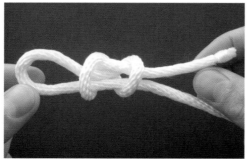

5. Adjust the piece, and then flip it over. The long end should be on the bottom.

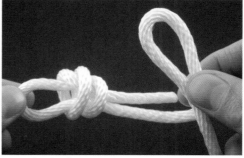

6. Bight the long end…